THE STAR WARS® COOK BOOK

►WOOKIEE COOKIES

AND OTHER GALACTIC RECIPES BY ROBIN DAVIS

PHOTOGRAPHY BY FRANKIE FRANKENY

chronicle books · san francisco

Copyright © 1998 Lucasfilm Ltd. & ®
All rights reserved. Used under authorization.
Published by Chronicle Books.
www.starwars.com

Figures and vehicles courtesy of Hasbro, Galoob, and Applause.

Heath® Milk Chocolate English Toffee Bar is a registered trademark of the Hershey Foods Corporation.
Jell-O® is a registered trademark of Kraft Foods, Inc.
Kit Kat® is a registered trademark of the H.B. Reese Candy Company.

Book design by Daniel Carter/STUDIO 212.
Art direction and concepts by Frankie Frankeny and Wesley Martin.
Styling by Wesley Martin.
Typeset in Bell Gothic, Clicker, and Univers.
Printed in Malaysia.

Library of Congress Cataloging-in-Publication Data available
ISBN 978-0-8118-2184-1

20 19 18 17 16 15 14 13 12 11
Chronicle Books
680 Second Street, San Francisco, California 94107

www.chroniclekids.com

Table of Contents

Introduction

Consider, young Jedi: Why bake a plain old cookie when you can bake a super-Chewie Wookiee Cookie?

The Force inhabits all realms, including the kitchen. Its power is as present in the refrigerator as it is on the desolate ice planet Hoth. *The Star Wars Cookbook* is your guide to cooking with the Force.

Some of these recipes are easy enough to make on your own and share with friends. For others, you will need the help of a grown-up. Definitely get your parents or other adults involved. Many moms and dads are masters of the Force who are lying low for mysterious reasons. Seek the wisdom of their cooking experience.

For Rebels in a time crunch, there are plenty of ideas here for whipping up good food in a hurry. In many cases, twenty minutes—about the time it takes to vanquish an ice creature or rid your ship of cable-chewing mynocks—is all you need to put a wholesome meal on the table.

As you journey into the dangers of the kitchen, you will want the wisdom of *The Star Wars Cookbook* to help you find your way. Adventure awaits as you develop the skills you need to bring the life force of food to all who hunger for it. Accept the challenge, young Rebel, and feel the Force!

GETTING STARTED

Before you start cooking, you must master some essential safety steps. The kitchen is a realm of peace, yet danger lurks in the most ordinary-seeming places. The two most important rules to remember are:

1. Keep an adult in the kitchen at all times, especially when you use knives, the stovetop, or the oven. Adults make good company and are helpful and handy to have around. (Even Luke would have been toast without Ben Kenobi to guide and protect him.) They can reach high places, drive, use the phone, pay, and offer valuable advice. Remember, never use anything sharp or hot without an adult to guide you.

2. Wash your hands with soap and warm water before cooking. You remember the hideous creatures in the Mos Eisley Cantina? They are nothing compared to what are crawling around on your hands. Fight those microscopic life forms with your best weapons: soap and water. It's a good idea to wash your hands a few times while you're cooking, too, as the germ troops are known to send in constant reinforcements.

The calm and perceptive mind of a Jedi warrior will enable you to prevent most mishaps in the kitchen. Use it well and follow these general guidelines:

BE CAREFUL
Respect the mysteries of The Force
► Never run in the kitchen.
► Keep everything—pot holders, towels, packages of ingredients, this book—away from burners on the stove. The stove can be hot even if the burners are all turned off.
► Dry your hands before turning on any electric switch or putting in or pulling out a plug.
► Wash knives and other sharp utensils one at a time. Don't drop them in a pan or bucket of soapy water—you may cut yourself when you reach in to fish them out.
► Lift lids on hot pots at an angle away from you, directing the rising steam away from your face.
► Use only dry pot holders. Wet ones will give you a steam burn when you touch the handle

of a hot pot.
► Put a pot or pan on the stove before you turn on the heat.
► Turn off the heat before you remove a pot or pan from the stove.
► Never put out a grease fire with water. Water causes grease to splatter and can spread the fire very quickly. To put out a grease fire, smother it with a tight fitting lid or throw handfuls of baking soda onto it.

BE AWARE
Cultivate the awareness of a Jedi
► Never leave the kitchen while something is cooking on the stove or in the oven.
► Keep pot handles away from the edge of the stove so no one passing by topples the pot.
► Always position pot handles away from other stove burners. They'll get hot and burn you when you go to move the pot.
► Remove utensils from hot pots when you're not using them, placing them on a plate or spoon holder near the stove. Metal spoons and spatulas are especially dangerous, because they'll absorb and hold the heat and burn your hand when you go to use them.
► Start with a clean kitchen and keep it clean as you cook. When something spills, wipe it up immediately to keep accidents from happening. If you have time, wash dishes as you go.
► Turn off the blender's motor before removing the lid.

► Put ingredients away when you're finished with them.
► Know where to find the fire extinguisher and be sure it's in working order.
► Keep the fire department number next to the phone.

The tools of a Wookiee Cookie chef are powerful but simple. You probably already have everything in your kitchen. Here's an alphabetical list of what you may need.

EQUIPMENT
Aluminum foil
Baking dishes
Baking sheets
Blender*
Can opener
Candy thermometer*
Cheese grater
Colander
Cooling rack
Cutting board
Electric mixer*

Ice cream scoop
Ice-cube tray
Knives* (one large and one small)
Measuring cups and spoons
Mixing bowls of various sizes
Paper cups
Pastry brush
Plastic wrap
Popsicle Sticks
Potato masher
Pot holders
Rolling pin
Rubber and metal spatulas
Saucepans with lids
Sieve
Sifter
Skewers*
Skillet
Star-shaped cookie cutters
Tea kettle
Toaster oven*
Toothpicks
Vegetable peeler
Wax paper
Whisk
Wooden spoons

*Use these items with extreme caution. Definitely get an adult to assist you any time you need to use them.

Go forth, young Jedi! May your Hoth Chocolate be sweet, may your Dark Side Salsa be spicy, and may the Force always be with you!

Breakfasts

Princess Leia Danish Dos

INGREDIENTS

Butter for greasing baking sheet

All-purpose flour for dusting work surface

1 tablespoon butter

1 10-oz package refrigerator pizza dough

2 tablespoons granulated sugar

$1\frac{1}{2}$ teaspoons ground cinnamon

1 tablespoon milk

$\frac{1}{3}$ cup confectioners' sugar, sifted

$\frac{1}{4}$ teaspoon vanilla extract

1. Preheat the oven to 350°F. Lightly grease a baking sheet.
2. Put the 1 tablespoon butter in a small saucepan. Set the pan on the stove and switch on the heat to low. When the butter has melted, turn off the heat.
3. Lightly flour a work surface. Unroll the pizza dough on top of the flour. Using a pastry brush, brush the melted butter over the surface of the dough.
4. Put the granulated sugar and cinnamon in a small bowl. Stir with a small spoon until well mixed. Sprinkle the cinnamon-sugar mixture over the dough, leaving a $\frac{1}{2}$-inch border on all sides.
5. Starting at a long side, roll up the dough into a log. Using your fingertips, pinch the seam together to seal.
6. Using a knife, cut the log crosswise into 1-inch-thick slices. Put the slices, cut side up, onto the greased baking sheet.
7. Using pot holders, put the baking sheet in the preheated oven. Bake until golden brown, about 20 minutes. Carefully transfer the baking sheet to the cooling rack. Cool 5 minutes. With a spatula, transfer rolls to the cooling rack and cool five minutes more.
8. Put the milk and confectioners' sugar in a small bowl. Stir with the spoon until a smooth frosting forms. Stir in the vanilla. Using a butter knife, spread frosting over the tops of the cinnamon rolls.
Makes about 10 rolls.

C-3PO Pancakes

INGREDIENTS

5	tablespoons unsalted butter
2	cans (8 1/4-ounces each) pineapple rings
1 1/4	cups all-purpose flour
2	tablespoons brown sugar
2	teaspoons baking powder
1/2	teaspoon salt
2	large eggs
1	cup milk
	Butter and maple syrup for serving

1. Preheat the oven to 250°F.

2. Put the butter in a small saucepan and switch on the heat to low. When the butter has melted, turn off the heat. Let the butter cool slightly (5 minutes).

3. Meanwhile, open the cans of pineapple. Drain off the juice from the cans into the sink. Set aside.

4. Put the flour, brown sugar, baking powder, and salt in a large bowl. Stir with a wooden spoon until well mixed.

5. Break the eggs into a medium bowl. Add the milk and 4 tablespoons of the melted butter. Whisk until well mixed. Slowly whisk in the flour mixture until well blended.

6. With a pastry brush, lightly brush some of the remaining melted butter in a large skillet. Set the skillet on the stove and switch on the heat to medium-high.

7. Fill a 1/3-cup measuring cup with batter. When the skillet is hot, after 1 minute or so, pour in the batter. Cook the pancake until golden underneath and bubbles burst on the top, about 3 minutes.

8. Place 1 pineapple ring in the center of the pancakes. Using a spatula, carefully flip the pancake. Cook until golden brown on the second side, about 2 minutes longer. Transfer the pancake to a baking sheet. Using pot holders, put the sheet in the oven.

9. Repeat steps 7 and 8, brushing skillet with butter as needed. Serve the pancakes warm with butter and maple syrup.

Makes 8 pancakes.

Oola-la French Toast

INGREDIENTS

1	egg
¼	cup milk
1½	teaspoons sugar
⅛	teaspoon vanilla extract
¼	teaspoon cinnamon, or a pinch of ground cloves
3	bread slices
3	teaspoons butter
	Confectioners' sugar (optional)
	Butter and maple syrup for serving

1. Preheat the oven to 250°F.
2. Break the egg into a bowl. Add the milk, sugar, vanilla, and cinnamon or cloves. Beat with a whisk until blended. Pour into a shallow dish such as a pie pan.
3. Put bread slices into the egg mixture. Let sit for a few moments. With your fingers, turn the bread over and again let sit for a few moments. Both sides should look soaked with the egg mixture.
4. Put 1 teaspoon butter in a skillet. Put the skillet on the stove and switch on the heat to medium-high.
5. When the butter melts, pick up one piece of soaked bread and put it into the pan. Be careful not to burn your fingers. Fry until golden brown on the underside, about 3 minutes. To check, lift a corner with a spatula, and take a peek. If ready, use the spatula to turn it over. Now fry until golden brown on the second side, about 2 minutes longer.
6. With the spatula, move the toast to a baking sheet. Using pot holders, put the sheet in the oven.
7. Repeat steps 4, 5, and 6 to cook the remaining French toast.
8. Remove the sheet from the oven. (Don't forget to use the pot holders!) If desired, sprinkle the French toast with confectioners' sugar. Serve hot with butter and maple syrup.
Makes 1 or 2 servings.

Twin Sun Toast

Tattooine is a hot desert planet located in the outer reaches of the galaxy. It is home to young Luke Skywalker, who would sometimes gaze dreamily at the planet's twin suns.

INGREDIENTS

1	wide slice sourdough bread (at least 7 inches wide)
1	teaspoon butter
2	small eggs
	Salt and pepper to taste

1. Put the bread slice on a cutting board. Using a 2-inch round cookie cutter, cut out 2 holes, side by side, in the bread. Make sure to leave bread between and around holes.
2. Put a skillet on the stove and switch on the heat to medium. Put the butter in the skillet.
3. As the butter melts, spread it evenly on the bottom of the pan. Place the bread slice in the pan and break an egg into each hole. Sprinkle a little salt and pepper on the eggs. Fry until the clear part of the eggs turn white, 1 to 2 minutes.
4. Slip a spatula under the bread and flip it over quickly but carefully. Don't let the eggs slip out of the holes. Cook for 1 minute more. Slide the toast onto a plate. Serve at once.
Makes 1 serving.

Mos Eisley Morsels

INGREDIENTS

	Butter for greasing baking dish
2	cups all purpose flour
2	teaspoons baking powder
1/2	teaspoon baking soda
1 1/2	teaspoons ground cinnamon
1	teaspoon ground nutmeg
1/2	teaspoon ground cloves
1/4	teaspoon salt
3	large bananas
1	large egg
2	tablespoons vegetable oil
2	teaspoons vanilla

1. Preheat the oven to 375°F.
2. Lightly grease an 8-inch square baking dish.
3. Put the flour, baking powder, baking soda, cinnamon, nutmeg, cloves, and salt into a sifter. Sift the ingredients into large bowl.
4. In another large bowl, thoroughly mash the bananas with a fork or potato masher. Add the egg, vegetable oil, and vanilla, and stir until well blended.
5. Add the flour mixture and with a rubber spatula, mix the wet and dry ingredients together until just combined.
6. Pour the batter into the prepared baking dish and smooth the top of the batter with the spatula.
7. Using pot holders, place the baking dish in the oven and bake for 30-35 minutes, until a toothpick inserted into the center comes out clean. Using pot holders, transfer the dish to a cooling rack. Cut into squares.
Makes 12 morsels.

Variations: The morsels in the picture are topped with an extra mashed banana. If desired, mash a banana in a separate bowl, and spread on squares just before eating. Do not top the morsels with mashed banana unless you're going to eat them right away!

Beverages

Hoth Chocolate

Skywalker Smoothies

Jawa Jive Milkshakes

Yoda Soda

Hoth Chocolate

The Rebellion's hidden Echo Base on the ice planet Hoth was freezing! Sometimes the Rebels wished they could just warm up with a mug of this Hoth chocolatey drink.

INGREDIENTS

1	cup milk
2	heaping teaspoons sugar
1	heaping teaspoon unsweetened cocoa powder
1/8	teaspoon vanilla extract
	Small marshmallows (optional)

1. Pour the milk into a small saucepan. Add the sugar, cocoa powder, and vanilla to the milk. Stir vigorously with a whisk until the sugar and cocoa dissolve.

2. Place the pan on the stove and switch on the heat to medium. Watch for tiny bubbles to appear along the edge of the pan, then immediately remove the pan from the heat.

3. Carefully pour into the mug and serve immediately with marshmallows, if desired.

Makes 1 serving.

kywalker Smoothies

Luke definitely has the Force on his side, but sometimes he gets an extra boost from these scrumptious smoothies.

INGREDIENTS

1	cup fresh or frozen strawberries
1	banana
½	cup pineapple, grape, or orange juice
4	ice cubes

1. If you are using fresh strawberries, cut off their stems with a knife. Put the fresh or frozen berries in a blender.
2. Peel the banana. Break it into pieces and add them to the blender. Then add the fruit juice and ice cubes.
3. Put the lid on the blender. Make sure it fits tightly. Turn on the blender first at low speed, then increase to high speed. Blend until smooth and frothy, 1 to 2 minutes. Turn off the blender and wait until it stops. With a wooden spoon, check to see that the fruit is thoroughly blended. If not, repeat this step.
4. Pour into 2 glasses and serve immediately.
Makes 2 servings.

Variation: Add a scoop of vanilla or berry frozen yogurt to the blender along with the other ingredients.

Jawa Jive Milkshakes

Jawas are famous for scavenging abandoned ships, droids, and scrap metal. When they get together at giant swap meets, they allegedly serve these delicious shakes.

CHOCOLATE-BANANA

- 2 cups vanilla ice cream or frozen yogurt
- 1 banana, peeled and broken into pieces
- $1/2$ cup milk
- $1/4$ cup chocolate syrup
- $1/2$ cup crushed Heath® Bars (optional)

VANILLA AND PEANUT BUTTER

- 1 cups vanilla ice cream or frozen yogurt
- 1 teaspoon vanilla extract
- $1/2$ cup milk
- $1/4$ cup creamy peanut butter
- $1/2$ cup peanut butter chips

SUPER STRAWBERRY

- 2 cups strawberry ice cream or frozen yogurt
- 1 cup frozen strawberries
- $1/2$ cup milk
- $1/2$ cup white chocolate chips (optional)

DOUBLE CHOCOLATE

- 2 cups chocolate ice cream or frozen yogurt
- $1/2$ cup milk
- $1/4$ cup chocolate syrup
- $1/2$ cup crushed chocolate sandwich cookies (optional)

1. Select the milkshake you want to make. Assemble the ingredients for your recipe. (Tip: The best way to crush the cookies or candy bar is to put them in a clean, sturdy plastic bag and roll a rolling pin back and forth over them.)

2. Put all the ingredients into a blender.

3. Put the lid on the blender. Make sure it fits tightly. Turn on the blender first at low speed, then increase to high speed. Blend until smooth, 1 to 2 minutes.

4. Pour the milkshake into 2 glasses. Serve each shake with a spoon and a straw.

Makes 2 milkshakes.

Yoda Soda

Jedi Master Yoda levitates Luke's X-wing from the Dagobah swamp in *The Empire Strikes Back*. Here he peacefully levitates a frothy glass of Yoda Soda.

INGREDIENTS

3	limes
3	tablespoons sugar, or more to taste
1	cup sparkling water
1	scoop lime sherbet or sorbet

1. Place 1 lime on the cutting board and cut it in half. Squeeze the juice from each half into a measuring cup. Repeat with the remaining limes until you have ¼ cup juice.

2. Put the lime juice and 3 tablespoons sugar in a small pitcher. Stir with a wooden spoon until the sugar dissolves. Add the sparkling water and stir until mixed. Taste and add more sugar, if desired.

3. Using an ice cream scoop, scoop up the sherbet and drop it into a tall glass. Pour in the lime water. Serve immediately.

Makes 1 serving.

Variation: You can substitute rainbow sherbet or lemon sorbet for the lime sherbet.

Snacks and Sides

Dark Side Salsa

INGREDIENTS

6	ripe Roma tomatoes
1	small onion
1	small avocado
1	can (4 ounces) diced mild green chiles
1	cup frozen corn, thawed
1	lemon or lime
	Salt and pepper to taste
	Blue corn tortilla chips

1. Put a tomato on the cutting board and cut out the green stem. Cut the tomato in half from the top to the bottom. Holding a tomato half cut side down, slice it lengthwise into thin slices. Now cut the slices into little cubes. Put the tomato cubes in the mixing bowl. Repeat with the remaining tomatoes.

2. Put the onion on the cutting board. Carefully slice off the root end and the stem end. Strip off the dry brown skin. Then cut the onion in half from the top to the bottom. Holding an onion half cut side down, thinly slice it crosswise. Now hold the slices together and cut across them in the opposite direction. Be sure to keep your fingers clear of the knife blade. Add the onion to the tomatoes.

3. Pit the avocado by carefully cutting it in half around the pit. Pull the halves apart and carefully scoop out the pit with a spoon. Peel the skin from the avocado with your fingers. Place the avocado half cut side down on the cutting board. Cut it lengthwise into thin slices, then cut the slices into little cubes. Repeat with the remaining avocado half. Add the avocado to the tomatoes and onions.

4. Open the can of chiles. Drain off the liquid from the can into the sink. Add the chiles to the mixing bowl. Then add the thawed corn.

5. Put the lemon or lime on the cutting board and cut it in half. Hold a half in your hand and squeeze it over a tablespoon until the tablespoon is full of juice. Add the juice to the mixing bowl.

6. Stir together everything in the bowl until well mixed. Add the salt and pepper to taste. Serve with the tortilla chips.

Makes 4 servings.

Ewok Eats

INGREDIENTS

6	fresh herb sprigs, a combination of parsley, thyme, and chives
$\frac{1}{2}$	cup plain yogurt
4	ounces cream cheese, at room temperature
1	teaspoon Worcestershire sauce
$\frac{1}{4}$	teaspoon garlic salt
1	teaspoon pepper
1	head broccoli

1. With your fingers, pull the thyme and parsley leaves off the stems. Put the leaves and chives on the cutting board and carefully chop with a knife. Set aside.

2. Put the yogurt and cream cheese in the mixing bowl. Stir with the wooden spoon until smooth. Add the chopped herbs, Worcestershire sauce, salt, and pepper and stir well. Cover with plastic wrap and refrigerate for 1 hour to give the flavors time to blend.

3. Put the head of broccoli on the cutting board. Use the knife to cut off the florets (the flowery looking tops). Be sure to leave a little stem on the florets. If the florets are in big clusters, cut between the stems to make smaller ones.

4. Spread the dip in the bottom of a shallow dish such as a pie pan. Stand the florets upright in the dip, side by side to make an Ewok forest.

Makes 4 servings.

Variation: You can also serve the dip with potato chips, tortilla chips, or other vegetables such as carrot and celery sticks.

The Force Fruit Fun

INGREDIENTS

2	cups strawberries, bananas, or blueberries, or a combination of the three
2	teaspoons lemon juice
3	tablespoons sugar

1. Preheat oven to 225ºF.

2. Wash the fruit. Remove strawberry stems with a knife and peel the bananas, if using.

3. Place fruit in a blender. Put the lid on the blender. Make sure it fits tightly. Turn blender on low speed first, then up to high and puree until smooth. Turn off the blender. Add lemon juice and sugar. Put the lid on again and blend.

4. With a rubber spatula, spread the fruit puree as thinly as possible onto a non-stick baking sheet.

5. Bake in the oven for about 25 minutes.

6. Using a potholder, transfer the baking sheet to a cooling rack. Allow to cool, then peel the fruit off of the sheet and eat!

Makes 1-2 servings.

Tusken Raider Taters

Tusken Raiders are fierce, mysterious creatures who wander the Tatooine desert, climbing sand dunes that look mysteriously like these potato dunes.

INGREDIENTS

1	teaspoon salt
1	pound purple or russet potatoes
¼	cup milk
2	tablespoons butter
	Salt and pepper to taste

1. Fill a large saucepan two-thirds full with water. Add the salt.
2. Using the vegetable peeler, peel the potatoes. Put a peeled potato on the cutting board. Cut the potato in half lengthwise. Holding a potato half cut side down, slice it lengthwise into 1-inch slices. Now hold the slices and cut across them in the opposite direction to make 1-inch pieces. Be sure to keep your fingers clear of the knife blade. Add the potato to the pan. Repeat with the remaining potatoes.
3. Put the pan on the stove and switch on the heat to high. Bring the water to a boil and boil the potatoes, uncovered, until tender, about 10 minutes. (You can check by scooping out a potato cube with a slotted spoon, and poking the cube with a fork. It should go in easily.) Turn off the heat.
4. Put the colander in the sink. Remove the pan from the stove and pour the water and potatoes into the colander. Be very careful; the steam from the boiling water can burn you.
5. Return the potatoes to the pan. Mash with a potato masher. Add the milk and butter. Continue to mash until the butter and milk are mixed in. Potatoes can be as smooth or lumpy as you like. Season to taste with salt and pepper.
Makes 2 servings.

Variation: If you want brown potatoes like the ones in the picture, mash russet potatoes with 2 tablespoons of soy sauce.

Jabba Jiggle

This green, fruity treat wiggles and jiggles just like Jabba.

INGREDIENTS

1   can (11-ounces) mandarin orange segments

1   can (8-ounces) crushed pineapple in juice

1   package (6-ounces) lime Jell-O®

2   cups cold water

1   cup seedless grapes

1. Open the cans of mandarin oranges and crushed pineapple. Drain off the juice from the cans into the sink.

2. Fill a tea kettle with water. Put the kettle on the stove and switch on the heat to high. Bring the water to a boil and remove from the heat.

3. Open the Jell-O® package and empty it into a large mixing bowl. Carefully measure 2 cups boiling water and pour them over the Jell-O®. Stir with the wooden spoon until the Jell-O® dissolves completely. Then stir in the cold water.

4. Add the drained mandarin oranges, pineapple, and the grapes. Stir until well mixed.

5. Pour the mixture into a glass bowl. Refrigerate until firm, about 2 hours.

Makes 8 servings.

Jedi Juice Pops

INGREDIENTS

14   small fresh or frozen strawberries

1¼ cups fruit juice, such as orange, cranberry,
      apple, fruit punch, or lemonade

1. If you are using fresh strawberries, cut off their
stems with a small knife. Place 1 strawberry in
each ice-cube compartment of an ice-cube tray.
Fill the ice-cube tray with the juice.
2. Put the tray in the freezer and freeze until
almost firm, about 2 hours.
3. Push a popsicle stick (or a toothpick) into
the center of each cube, through the strawberry.
Return to the freezer and freeze until firm,
about 1 hour longer.
4. Pop out the juice bars and eat!
Makes 14 pops.

Variation: You can use banana slices, seedless
grapes, or orange segments cut into chunks
instead of strawberries.

Main Courses

Greedo's Burritos

Han-burgers

Obi-Wan Kebabs

Galaxy Grilled Cheese

Boba Fett-uccine

Crazy Cantina Chili

TIE Fighter Ties

Greedo's Burritos

INGREDIENTS

1	can (14-ounces) black beans
1	cup grated Monterey Jack cheese
1/2	head iceberg lettuce
1	tomato
1	tablespoon olive oil or vegetable oil
1 1/2	pounds lean ground beef
4	flour tortillas, each about 10 inches in diameter
1/2	cup sliced black olives

1. Get an adult to help you with this recipe!

2. Preheat oven to 350°F.

3. Open the can of beans and drain the liquid into the sink. Set aside.

4. Put the iceberg lettuce on the cutting board cut side down. Cut the lettuce from top to bottom in narrow slices. Now cut across the slices, again in narrow strips. Set aside.

5. Put the tomato on the cutting board. Cut out the green stem. Then cut the tomato in half from the top to the bottom. Holding a tomato half cut side down, slice it crosswise about ½-inch thick. Now cut the slices into little cubes. Set aside.

6. Put the oil in a skillet. Put the skillet on the stove and switch on the heat to medium high. When the oil is hot, carefully add the beef. Cook, stirring often, until browned, about 15 minutes.

7. Wrap the tortillas in aluminum foil and place in the oven to heat, about 5 to 10 minutes.

8. Meanwhile, add the beans to the beef and continue to cook, stirring often, until the beans are heated through, about 2 minutes. Turn off the heat.

9. Using pot holders, remove tortillas from the oven. Place a tortilla on a plate. Spoon one-fourth of the beef mixture onto the tortilla. Sprinkle with one-fourth of the cheese. Top with one-fourth each of the olives, the tomato, and the lettuce. Roll up the tortilla around the filling.

10. Repeat step 9 until all the ingredients are used up.

Makes 4 burritos.

Han-Burgers

Han Solo is generally right-handed, but is known to fire a ketchup blaster with his left hand. (Condiments always taste better when blasted onto one's food.)

INGREDIENTS

1	pound ground lean beef
1	teaspoon salt
$1/2$	teaspoon pepper
1	teaspoon Worcestershire sauce
4	tomato slices
4	whole-wheat hamburger buns
	Lettuce leaves, pickle slices, ketchup, and mustard for serving

1. Put the ground beef, salt, pepper and Worcestershire sauce in a bowl. Using your hands, mix them together until well blended.

2. Divide the meat mixture in 8 equal portions. Form the portions into 8 patties $1/4$-inch-thick.

3. Place 1 tomato slice on 1 patty. Top with another patty. Use your fingers to press the edges together to seal. Repeat this step to make 4 filled patties.

4. Put a large skillet on the stove and switch on the heat to medium. When the skillet is hot, after about 1 minute or so, carefully put the hamburgers in the pan. Cook until browned on the underside, about 6 minutes. To check, lift a corner of the burger with the spatula and peak underneath. Flip over the hamburger and cook on the second side until browned and cooked through, about 6 minutes longer.

5. Use the spatula to transfer the burger onto the bun. Serve with lettuce leaves, pickle slices, ketchup, and mustard—blasted on, of course!

Makes 4 Han-burgers.

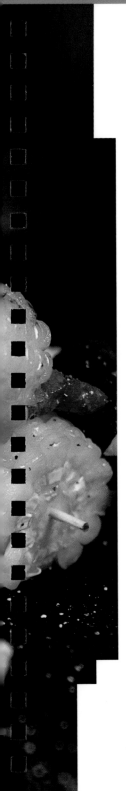

Obi-Wan Kebabs

INGREDIENTS

2	chicken breasts
4	small red new potatoes
3	zucchinis
3	ears of corn
	Olive oil

1. Get an adult to help you with this recipe!

2. Soak 8 wooden skewers in water for 30 minutes.

3. Preheat the oven to 375°F.

4. Put a chicken breast on a cutting board. Using a knife, cut the meat in 1-inch strips. Now cut across the strips to make 1-inch cubes. Repeat with remaining chicken breast. Set chicken aside.

5. Wash the cutting board and knife thoroughly with soap and warm water. Rinse and dry the cutting board.

6. Put a small potato on the cutting board and cut it in half. Repeat with remaining potatoes and set aside.

7. Put a zucchini on the cutting board. Trim off the stem and the base. Then cut the zucchini into 1-inch rounds. Repeat with the remaining zucchini and set aside.

8. Put an ear of corn on the cutting board. Cut the corn into 1-inch rounds. Repeat with remaining corn.

9. Very carefully push one round of corn onto the skewer. Follow with a potato half, chicken cube, and zucchini slice. Begin again with the corn and continue until there are only 2 inches left on the skewer.

10. Using a pastry brush, brush the meat and vegetables with olive oil and sprinkle with salt and pepper.

11. Grill or broil until vegetables are tender and chicken is cooked through, turning frequently, about 30 minutes.

Makes 8 kebabs.

Galaxy Grilled Cheese

INGREDIENTS

4	slices whole-wheat bread
4	teaspoons butter, at room temperature
8	thin slices Cheddar cheese
8	pickle slices

1. Lay 1 slice of bread on a work surface. Spread one side with 1 teaspoon of the butter. Repeat with the remaining bread slices and butter.

2. Turn 2 bread slices over so the buttered sides are down. Top the slices with the cheese slices, dividing them evenly.

3. Lay 4 pickle slices on top of each stack of cheese. Top with the other 2 bread slices, buttered sides up.

4. Place the sandwiches in a skillet. Set the skillet on the stove and switch on the heat to medium. Cook the sandwiches until golden brown on the underside and the cheese begins to melt, about 3 minutes. To check, lift up a corner of a sandwich with a spatula and peek underneath. Using the spatula, flip over both sandwiches. Cook until golden brown on the second side and the cheese has melted, about 3 minutes longer.

5. Use the spatula to transfer the sandwiches to a cutting board. You can cut your sandwiches into stars or planets if you have a star-shaped or round cookie cutter. Press the cookie cutter straight down into the sandwich. Be careful not to burn your fingers on the hot cheese. Lift the cutter gently. Repeat with the other sandwich. Serve the sandwiches immediately.

Makes 2 sandwiches.

Boba Fett-uccine

INGREDIENTS

1	small head broccoli		$1^{1}/_{2}$	cups bottled pasta sauce
1	small head cauliflower		3	quarts water
1	small zucchini		$^{1}/_{2}$	pound fettuccine noodles
3	teaspoons salt			Grated Parmesan cheese

1. Put the broccoli on a cutting board. Using a knife, cut off the florets (the flowery-looking tops). Measure one cup of florets. Repeat this step with the cauliflower.

3. Put the zucchini on the cutting board. Trim off the stem and the base. Then cut the zucchini into thin rounds.

4. Fill a medium saucepan three-fourths full with water. Add 1 $^{1}/_{2}$ teaspoons of the salt. Put the pan on the stove and switch on the heat to high. When the water boils, slowly add broccoli, cauliflower, and zucchini. Cook until tender, about 4 minutes.

5. Turn off the heat. Place colander in the sink. Remove the pan from the stove and pour the water and vegetables into the colander. Be very careful; steam can burn you.

6. Return the vegetables to the saucepan. Pour in the pasta sauce. Set the pan on the stove and switch on the heat to medium. Heat, stirring occasionally with a wooden spoon, until hot. Turn down the heat to very low.

7. Now pour the 3 quarts water into a large saucepan. Add the remaining 1 $^{1}/_{2}$ teaspoons salt. Put the pan on the stove and switch on the heat to high. When the water boils, slowly add the fettuccine and stir once or twice with a wooden spoon. Boil until tender, about 8 minutes or according to package directions.

8. Turn off the heat. Remove the pan from the stove and carefully pour the water and pasta into the colander.

9. Transfer the noodles to a large serving bowl. Pour the sauce over the top. Sprinkle with Parmesan cheese and serve.

Makes 2 to 3 servings.

Crazy Cantina Chili

INGREDIENTS

1	can (16-ounces) kidney beans
1	can (16-ounces) black beans
1	can (16-ounces) garbanzo beans
1	onion
2	tablespoons vegetable oil
2	tablespoons chili powder
1/8	teaspoon cayenne pepper
1	can (28-ounces) crushed tomatoes with juice
1	cup tomato juice
	Salt and pepper to taste
	Shredded Cheddar cheese
	Sour cream or plain yogurt

1. Open the cans of beans. Drain off the liquid from the cans into the sink. Set the beans aside.

2. Put the onion on a cutting board. Carefully slice off the root end and the stem end. Use your fingers to strip off the dry skin. Then cut the onion in half from the top to the bottom. Hold an onion half cut side down and thinly slice it crosswise. Now hold the slices together and cut across them in the opposite direction. Be sure to keep your fingers clear of the knife blade. Set aside.

3. Put the oil in a large saucepan. Set the pan on the stove and switch on the heat to medium-high. When the oil is hot, add the chopped onion and stir with the wooden spoon until tender, about 5 minutes.

4. Add the chili powder and cayenne pepper and stir for 30 seconds.

5. Add the beans, the crushed tomatoes, and the tomato juice. Stir well. Reduce heat to medium low and simmer for 15 minutes, stirring occasionally. Season to taste with salt and pepper.

6. Serve the chili with the cheese and sour cream on the side.

Makes 4 to 6 servings.

TIE Fighter Ties

These galactical finger-foods are sure to start a battle in your very own kitchen: a battle over who takes command of the fresh-from-the-oven fleet of TIE Fighter Ties!

INGREDIENTS

4	pre-cooked sausages or hotdogs, approximately 5-inches long
1	package refrigerator breadsticks (8 breadsticks)
	Ketchup and mustard

1. Preheat the oven to 350°F.
2. Cut sausages in half crosswise. Set aside.
3. Open the package of breadsticks and separate the lengths of dough.
4. Cut the lengths in half and set aside. You should have 16 lengths of dough when you are finished.
5. Place one sausage half, cut-side down, on a baking sheet.
6. Take 1 length of dough and wrap it around the base of the sausage half. Cross the ends and let them fall on the baking sheet in the form of the letter V. Using another length of dough, wrap the same sausage in the opposite direction. Cross the ends and let them fall in the form of an upside-down V. Repeat with remaining dough and sausage halves.
7. Bake according to breadstick package directions, or until dough puffs up and turns golden brown.
8. Using pot holders, remove from the oven. Serve with ketchup and mustard.

Makes 8 TIE Fighter Ties.

Desserts

Darth Vader Dark Chocolate Sundaes

Some speculate that Darth Vader was lured to the Dark Side by these Dark Chocolate Sundaes.

INGREDIENTS

$1/2$ cup bottled hot fudge sauce

1   quart chocolate ice cream

$1/2$ cup whipped cream

4   tablespoons chopped nuts

4   teaspoons chocolate chips or chocolate sprinkles

1. Put the hot fudge sauce in a small, heavy saucepan. Put the pan on the stove and switch on the heat to low. Stir constantly until the sauce is melted and smooth. Remove from the heat.

2. Set out 4 bowls. Put 2 scoops of ice cream into each bowl.

3. Top each serving with about 2 tablespoons hot fudge. Top with the whipped cream and sprinkle each serving with 1 tablespoon nuts and 1 teaspoon chocolate chips or sprinkles.

Makes 4 servings.

Variations: You can use any flavor ice cream or sauce that you like. Other toppings besides peanuts might include M&Ms, mini marshmallows, fresh berries, or shredded coconut.

Wookiee Cookies

INGREDIENTS

2 ¼ cups all-purpose flour

1   teaspoon baking soda

1   teaspoon salt

1   teaspoon ground cinnamon

1   cup unsalted butter, at room temperature

1   cup packed brown sugar

½   cup granulated sugar

2   large eggs

1 ½ teaspoons vanilla extract

1   cup milk chocolate chips

1   cup semi-sweet chocolate chips

1. Preheat the oven to 375°F.

2. Put the flour, baking soda, salt, and cinnamon in a mixing bowl. Stir with the wooden spoon until well mixed. Set aside.

3. Put the butter, brown sugar, and granulated sugar in another mixing bowl. Using the electric mixer set on high speed, beat together until well blended and creamy, about 3 minutes. (You can do this with a wooden spoon, but it will take longer.) Beat in the eggs and vanilla extract. Add the flour mixture and stir with the wooden spoon until blended. Stir in the chocolate chips.

4. Scoop up a rounded tablespoonful of the dough and drop onto a baking sheet. Repeat until you have used up all the dough. Be sure to leave about 1 inch between the cookies because they spread as they bake.

5. Using pot holders, put the baking sheets in the oven. Bake until golden brown, about 10 minutes.

6. Again, using pot holders, remove the baking sheets from the oven. Lift the cookies from the baking sheets with a spatula, and place on cooling racks. Let cool completely.

Makes about 3 dozen cookies.

Bossk Brownies

Bossk the bounty hunter never caught his quarry, Han Solo and Chewbacca. Perhaps he was distracted by these delicious brownies.

INGREDIENTS

	Butter for greasing baking dish
2/3	cup all-purpose flour
1/2	cup unsweetened cocoa powder
1/2	teaspoon baking powder
1/2	teaspoon salt
1/2	cup unsalted butter, at room temperature
1/2	cup packed brown sugar
1/2	cup granulated sugar
2	large eggs
1	teaspoon vanilla extract
1/2	cup white chocolate or butterscotch chips

1. Preheat the oven to 350°F. Butter an 8-inch square baking dish.
2. Put the flour, cocoa powder, baking powder, and salt in a small bowl. Stir with a wooden spoon until well mixed. Set aside.
3. Put the butter, brown sugar, and granulated sugar in one large bowl. Using the electric mixer set on high speed, beat together until well blended and creamy, about 3 minutes. (You can do this with the wooden spoon, but it will take longer.) Beat in the eggs and vanilla extract. Add the flour mixture and stir with the wooden spoon until blended. Stir in the white chocolate or butterscotch chips.
4. Pour into the prepared baking dish and smooth the top with a rubber spatula.
5. Using pot holders, put the baking dish in the preheated oven. Bake until a toothpick inserted into the center comes out clean, about 25 minutes.
6. Again using pot holders, transfer the dish to the cooling rack. Let cool completely.
Makes about 16 brownies.

Death Star Popcorn Balls

Like the Empire's deadly Death Star, making popcorn balls can be very dangerous. Do not dare to make them without the help of an adult.

INGREDIENTS

1/3 cup popcorn kernels	1 teaspoon vinegar
3 cups sugar	1 teaspoon vanilla extract
1 1/2 cups water	Butter or vegetable shortening for greasing hands
1/2 cup light corn syrup	
1/2 tablespoon salt	

1. Get an adult to help you with this recipe!
2. Pop the corn using whatever method you prefer.
3. Put the sugar, water, corn syrup, and salt in the saucepan. Stir well with a wooden spoon. Clip a candy thermometer on the side of the pan. Set the pan on the stove and switch on the heat to low. Add the vinegar and vanilla and cook, stirring constantly, until the thermometer reads 270°F.
4. Get an adult to carefully pour the hot sugar mixture over the popcorn and toss with two large spoons to coat every kernel. Allow to cool slightly.
5. Rub butter or vegetable shortening on your hands so the popcorn won't stick to them. Then scoop up enough popcorn to form a ball about the size of a baseball.
6. Shape the ball with your hands.
Makes 2 to 3 popcorn balls.

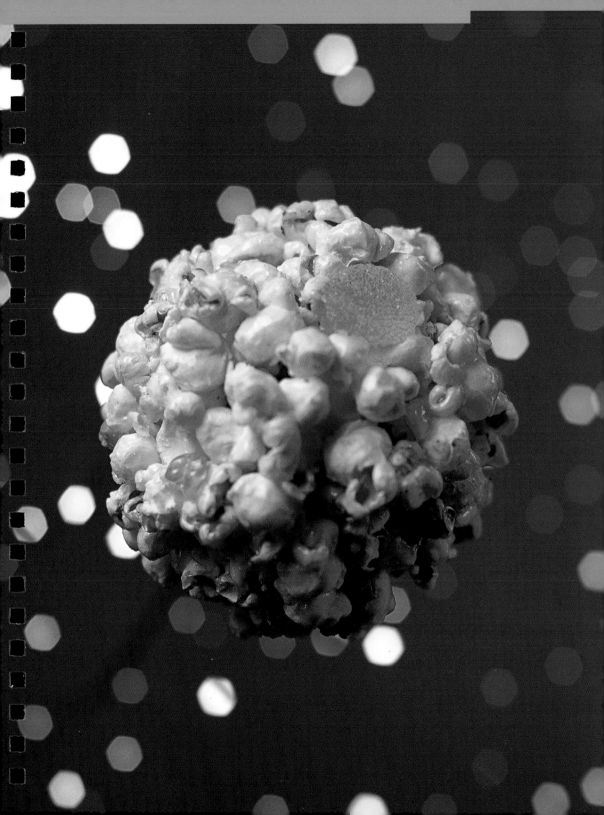

Wampa Snow Cones

Luke was imprisoned by a ferocious wampa on the ice planet Hoth, and held captive in the creature's frozen lair. Narrowly escaping with his life, some believe Luke also made off with the wampa's secret snow cone recipe.

INGREDIENTS

2	cups fresh or thawed frozen blueberries
¼	cup water
1	tablespoon sugar

1. Put the blueberries in a bowl. Mash them with a fork until there's lots of liquid.

2. Hold a strainer over a small glass baking dish and pour the mashed berries into a sieve. Press the berries with a fork to push through as much liquid as possible.

3. Add the water and sugar to the blueberry juice. With a wooden spoon, stir until the sugar dissolves. Put the dish in the freezer.

4. After 30 minutes take the dish out of the freezer. Stir the mixture with a fork to break up the crystals. Return the dish to the freezer for another 30 minutes.

5. Remove the dish again and break up the crystals one more time. Return to the freezer and freeze until firm, about 4 hours.

6. Remove the dish from the freezer. Using the fork, scrape the mixture into small crystals. Quickly scoop the crystals into small paper cups and serve right away.

Makes 2 servings.

Variation: Replace the blueberries, water, and sugar with a bottled fruit juice or drink such as apple juice, lemonade or punch. Follow the directions for freezing and scraping the crystals.

R2-D2 Treats

R2-D2 never eats, or so it seems. These frozen treats were discovered in a freezer at the abandoned Rebel base on Hoth. Did they belong to R2-D2? We can only guess...

INGREDIENTS

1/2	cup white chocolate chips
2	tablespoons chopped peanuts
1	banana
1	Kit Kat® candy bar

1. Line a baking sheet with waxed paper.
2. Put the chocolate chips in a small, heavy saucepan. Put the pan on the stove and switch on the heat to low. Stir constantly until the chocolate is melted and smooth. Remove from heat and set aside.
3. Peel the banana. Put on a cutting board and cut into 4 equal pieces.
4. Place the peanuts in a small bowl. Break the Kit Kat® into four bars. Cut each bar in half and set aside.
5. Dip 1 banana piece in the melted chocolate. Dip just the top of the banana piece into the peanuts.
6. Place the banana piece nut side up on the lined baking sheet. Press 2 Kit Kat® pieces along either side of the banana.
7. Repeat steps 5 and 6 with the remaining banana pieces.
8. Place the baking sheet in the freezer until chocolate has hardened, about 15 minutes. Serve straight from the freezer.
Makes 1 or 2 treats.

Sandtrooper Sandies

INGREDIENTS

3/4   cup butter, at room temperature

1 1/4 cups sugar

2   eggs

1   teaspoon vanilla extract

2   cups all-purpose flour

1/4   teaspoon salt

       Vegetable oil for greasing the baking sheet

       Confectioners' sugar

1. Put the butter in a bowl. With an electric mixer set on high speed, beat the butter until soft and light in color.

2. Gradually add the sugar in a slow, steady stream, and beat until creamy and lemon yellow. Then add the eggs one at a time, beating well after each addition. Add the vanilla and stir just until blended.

3. Put the flour and salt into a sifter and sift them into a small bowl. Slowly add the flour mixture to the butter mixture, beating it in with the electric mixer on low speed until it is fully incorporated. The dough will become very stiff and you may have to knead the last bit of flour in by hand. With your hands, pat the dough into a ball and flatten the ball into a thick disk. Wrap the dough in plastic wrap and chill in the refrigerator for 1 hour.

4. Preheat an oven to 400°F. Lightly oil a baking sheet.

5. Remove dough from the refrigerator and unwrap. Dust your work surface with flour. With a rolling pin, roll out the dough 1/4-inch thick.

6. Using cookie cutters of any shape you like, cut cookies out of the dough. Carefully transfer the cookies to the oiled baking sheet, leaving a little space around each one. Gather up any dough scraps, roll them out again, and cut out more cookies.

7. Slip baking sheet into the oven and bake until cookies just begin to brown, 8 to 10 minutes. Using pot holders, carefully remove the baking sheet from the oven. Transfer the cookies to cooling racks with a spatula and allow them to cool. Sift a little confectioners' sugar over the cookies.

Makes about 3 dozen cookies.

Index